WILD READS

Whales

Peter Haswell

OXFORD
UNIVERSITY PRESS

This book belongs to:

OXFORD
UNIVERSITY PRESS

Great Clarendon Street, Oxford OX2 6DP
Oxford University Press is a department of the University of Oxford.
It furthers the University's objective of excellence in research, scholarship,
and education by publishing worldwide in

Oxford   New York

Auckland   Cape Town   Dar es Salaam   Hong Kong   Karachi
Kuala Lumpur   Madrid   Melbourne   Mexico City   Nairobi
New Delhi   Shanghai   Taipei   Toronto

With offices in

Argentina   Austria   Brazil   Chile   Czech Republic   France   Greece
Guatemala   Hungary   Italy   Japan   Poland   Portugal   Singapore
South Korea   Switzerland   Thailand   Turkey   Ukraine   Vietnam

Oxford is a registered trade mark of Oxford University Press
in the UK and in certain other countries

Text © Peter Haswell
Illustrations © Steve White
The moral rights of the author have been asserted

Database right Oxford University Press (maker)

This edition 2009

British Library Cataloguing in Publication Data

Data available

ISBN: 978-0-19-911934-9

1 3 5 7 9 10 8 6 4 2

Printed in China
Paper used in the production of this book is a natural,
recyclable product made from wood grown in sustainable forests.
The manufacturing process conforms to the environmental
regulations of the country of origin.

Contents

▶ The mighty sea monster

In the cold, grey ocean a mighty sea monster is swimming. It rises to the surface and its sleek body slips through the waves. A fine mist spouts from the blowhole on the top of its head.

Suddenly, it leaps high out of the water. Then it falls with a great crash, sending a huge spray of water into the air. The monster flips up its tail and dives once again into the depths of the ocean.

What is the name of this sea monster?

Its name is "*whale*".

humpback whale

▶ Whales are not fish

Whales are not fish. Like us, they are mammals. Like us, they have warm blood. Like us, whale mothers carry their babies inside them until they are born.

beluga whale
4.5 metres

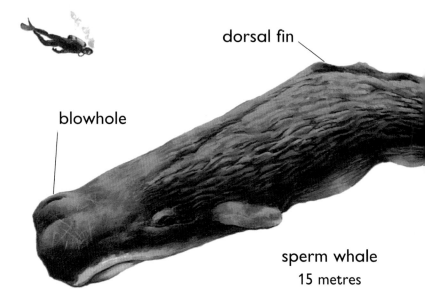

dorsal fin

blowhole

sperm whale
15 metres

right whale
14 metres

minke whale
8 metres

humpback whale
13 metres

tail flukes

Like us, whales cannot breathe underwater. They fill their lungs, close the blowhole on the top of their heads and dive. When they surface again they breathe out through their blowhole. The warm air forms a mist of spray above their heads.

sperm whale blowing

Did you know...
Most whales can stay underwater for about 40 minutes but sperm whales can stay under for up to two hours.

Like us, whales have long lives. The sperm whale can live to 70 and fin whales can even live until they are 90!

But of course, whales are also very different from us. They are born in the sea. They live in the sea. They find their food in the sea.

Did you know...
The bones in a whale's fin are like those in a human hand.

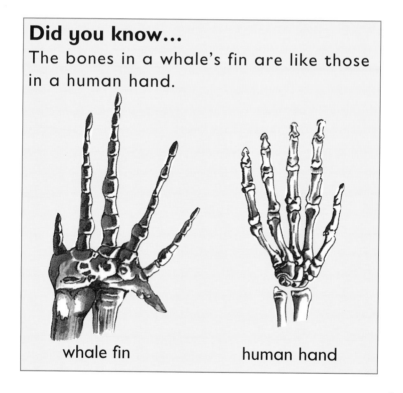

whale fin   human hand

Hunters and grazers

In the wild some animals, such as lions, are hunters that live by killing other creatures. Others are grazers, nibbling grass and plants all day long. Whales too are either hunters, called toothed whales, or grazers, called baleen whales.

sperm whale
(toothed whale)

Toothed whales

What they eat
Mainly fish and squid.
The sperm whale eats over
1,000 kilogrammes of
squid a day.

How they eat
Toothed whales have teeth
for catching their prey.

Some toothed whales

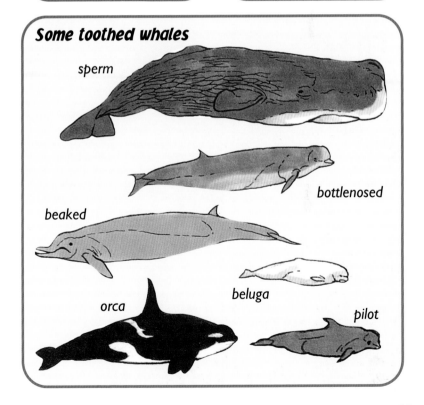

sperm

bottlenosed

beaked

beluga

orca

pilot

Baleen whales

What they eat
Millions and millions of tiny shrimp-like creatures called krill.

How they eat
Baleen whales do not have teeth. They have strips of whalebone called "baleen" (made of the same material as cows' horns and human fingernails).

The baleen hangs from the whale's upper jaw like a thick fringe. When feeding, the whale sucks in a massive mouthful of water containing millions of krill. It then squirts the water back out through the fringe of baleen. Imagine yourself squirting water out through your teeth.

The baleen then traps the krill in the whale's mouth – and so the whale can enjoy a feast.

bowhead whale
(baleen whale)

Some Baleen whales

blue

humpback

bryde's

sei

bowhead

grey

finback

minke

right

13

▶ Orca, the killer whale

The most fearsome toothed whale is the killer whale, orca. With its 44 sharp teeth, orca eats fish, penguins, seals, sharks – and other whales.

A pod of orcas

Orcas can swim as fast as a car driving along a street. They can leap as high as a double-decker bus.

Orcas live in family groups, called
pods, of up to 20. They often work as
a team when hunting.

A group of three hungry orcas is swimming through the Arctic Sea in search of food. They spot a seal sleeping on an ice floe.

Out of the water, the seal thinks it is safe. But it is not.

The three orcas split up. One sneaks to the end of the floe to wait.

The other two slide under the floe
and, suddenly, lift it upwards. The
startled seal wakes up – but too late.
The seal slides into the water and is
grabbed in the jaws of the waiting
orca.

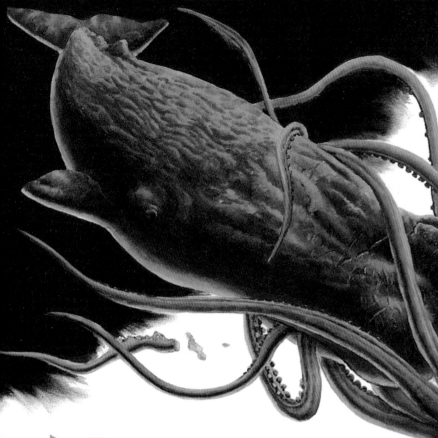

▶ The sperm whale's battle

The great sperm whale is another mighty hunter. It dives down to the bottom of the Atlantic Ocean and finds a giant squid. The squid is enormous – as long as a truck – and will be a satisfying meal for the hungry whale.

But it is also big enough to fight back.

A terrible battle takes place. The creatures struggle furiously, each fighting for its life.

At last, the sperm whale crushes the squid in its mighty jaws.

Now it must feed and return quickly to the surface to breathe again.

▶ The biggest animal ever

The biggest animal ever to live on earth is not a hunter. It is a baleen whale called the blue whale.

A newborn blue whale is as long as a motor boat. It drinks as much milk as 50 human families drink every day.

It takes the baby 30 years to grow to full size. It can live until it is 100.

Did you know...
The blue whale's tongue weighs as much as a baby elephant.

blue whale and calf

▶ Whale journeys

It is March and, off the coast of Mexico, over 1,000 grey whales are beginning to swim north. Their journey up the coast of America will take about three months.

As they swim, the whales will sometimes nudge and touch each other. From time to time, a mother will give her baby a piggyback.

Arriving in the Arctic they will stay until October, feeding on the rich supplies of krill. Then they will swim south again, returning to the warm waters of Mexico. Here they will breed during the winter months.

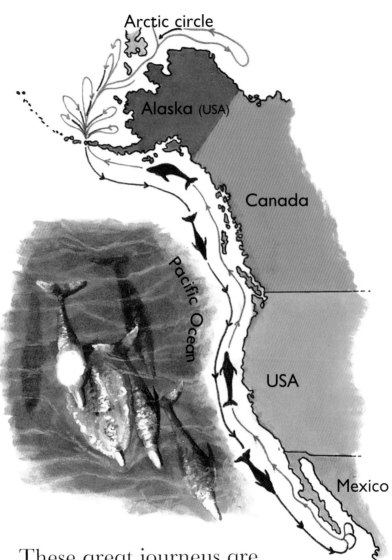

These great journeys are
called "migrations". Not all whales
migrate but, of those that do, the
grey whale is the greatest traveller.

▶ The song of the whale

Deep in the ocean whales sing to each other.

Their songs are a mixture of moans, grunts, sighs, whistles and other mysterious sounds.

male humpback whale in the head down singing position

Humpback whales are great singers. Sometimes a humpback will go on repeating its song for a whole day and night.

Why do whales sing? Nobody really knows. However, we do know that only males sing. It is thought they sing to attract mates, to let other whales know where they are and to warn rivals to keep away.

The whale's song is one of the strangest sounds on our planet. It is also one of the most beautiful.

Did you know...
If you shout to a friend half a kilometre away, he or she might just hear you.
A whale can be heard as much as 80 kilometres away.

human voice
whistle blown   humpback whale voice

| 0 km | 10 km | 20 km | 30 km | 40 km | 50 km | 60 km | 70 km | 80 km | 90 km |

▶ In danger

Every bit of a whale can be used.
So people have always hunted whales.

Once there were thousands of blue whales.

Now there are only a few thousand left in the whole world.

Whale hunting is now controlled.
But whales are still in danger.
We must make everyone aware that if the whale is not saved it will surely vanish from the earth.

The whale is the biggest animal in the world yet it can't defend itself against us.

humpback whale

In the cold blue ocean, a great and beautiful sea monster is swimming . . . it is the *mighty, wonderful whale!*

▶ Glossary

baleen Baleen is a fringe of whalebone that hangs from the upper jaws of those whales that have no teeth.   **10, 12, 13, 20**

blowhole A blowhole is a nostril on the top of a whale's head.   **4, 6, 8**

breed Breeding is when two whales mate and have a baby.

22

ice floe An ice floe is a flat piece of ice that floats like a raft on the sea in the oceans near the North and South Poles.   **16, 17**